Dear Dorothy and Sarah

I'm glad you read my book and found it interesting

Gill

15th January 2023

Braiswick
61 Gainsborough Road,
Felixstowe, Suffolk IP11 7HS

ISBN 1 898030 54 5

British Library Cataloguing in Publication
Data available.

Printed in Kent
by JRDigital Print Services Ltd
Braiswick is an imprint of Author Publishing Ltd

In Memory of
Ken Smith,
who died in May 2002.
He was the person who brought me back to life
with all his love and understanding
when I moved to Rusthall in 1995.

ACKNOWLEDGEMENTS

I have collected, written and designed
all this work by myself,
but I would never have managed to
compile this book without the help I have
received from my friend Rosie Davis
and Pam Nelson at COMPAID Trust.

I thank my parents for storing all the
material from my past,
which has become my roots.

I thank Anne Pilgrim, Bob Whyte,
Tony Rutherford, Rob Aylott
and all the other friends who
encouraged me to spread my work.

CONTENTS

INTRODUCTION

In 1982, a virus called Encephalitis attacked me. I was twenty-eight years old and had been working long hours, self-employed, engrossed in using graphic design to improve and express matters that I considered to be important information to society.

My illness overcame me with epileptic seizures and damaged both my long-term and my short-term memories. This meant that I had no memory of any time before my illness. All the knowledge I had accumulated at school, university and at work suddenly disappeared and I was left with just a disabled ability to create any new life.

Since then I have spent my time fighting epileptic seizures with my damaged brain.

Thankfully, I have saved some of my drawings and writing from childhood, which I am now able to use as a memory of myself. Also, I was encouraged to keep a diary during my illness, so that I can see for myself how I have improved, instead of just listening to other people trying to reassure me with the words, "You're looking so much better since I last saw you!"

So I have been able to restore self-confidence. This work is a present to myself from myself for my fiftieth birthday. It provides me with some roots for the growth of my future.

Humble yourself before the Lord and He will lift you up.

NT James 4:10

7

GS 1971

NOW in 2001

With a mind that seemed too damaged to use,
through branches that seemed too thick to hold,
up hills that seemed too steep to climb,
down paths that seemed too long to walk,
on rubble that seemed too coarse to stand on,
through mud that seemed too wet to wade through,
I find a place of peace, happiness, strength and change.
I don't feel frightened any more,
for fits are just a small part of me
and God has become real to me.
I can think well, making use of my old letters,
for they do provide proof of myself getting better.
I can find inspiration from new words to speak,
for they fill up the holes which were going to leak.
I can pick precious thoughts I do want to express,
instead of discarding them all in a mess.
The smallest of thoughts can count more today.
So I won't live in the past with the ones I can say.

MY FIRST WORDS
FATSY
YES
POVIL
DADDY
BREAD
BISEE

Mardi, 30 mai 1961

La locomotive traîne, tire les wagons. Elle a un panache de fumée; elle marche au charbon. Mon train est électrique. Je remonte le train mecanique avec une clé. Le train roule sur les rails, il suit la voie ferrée; s'il sort des rails, il déraille. L'employé de gare pousse le chariot – chargé de bagages sur le quai.

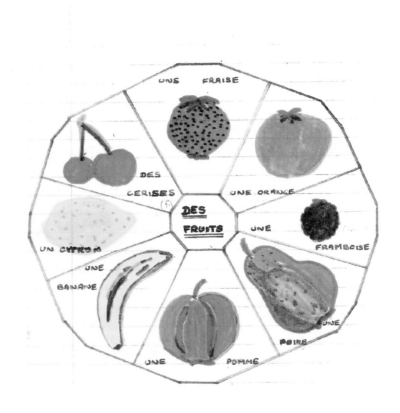

Making a pot of tea.

First I filled the kettle with some hot water and put it on the gas-stove. I turned on the gas and left the water to boil. While I was waiting I got out two cups and saucers and two teaspoons

Then I got the sugar out of the cupboard and the milk from the fridge. After that I filled the teapot with hot water, shook it, and poured the water into the sink. Next I put two teaspoonfuls tea into the teapot and poured the hot water into it. Later I put some milk and sugar into the cups, then poured the tea in. Finally I put the cups onto the tray and took them to my mother and father. ✓

13

7.2.63

Doing the washing up.

First I cleared the table, and rinsed all the dirty dishes and cutlery. Then I stacked everything up neatly by the side of the sink. Next I rolled up my sleeves, put my mother's plastic apron on, and set to work. I put some Fairy Liquid into the washing-up bowl, and filled it with warm water. After that I started to

wash the glasses, stacking them up neatly on the draining board, secondly I washed the cutlery, and last of all the crockery. Finally I dried them all with a dry cloth and put them away neatly.

14

The
Black
Forest
Mystery.

by Gillian Shaw

Chapter One
The Surprise

One day four children were looking out of the window at the pouring rain. It had been raining all day, and Mrs. Wilson their mother had found nothing for them to do. They left the window and started to rumble amongst their toys, when they heard a shout from downstairs. "John, Elizabeth, Mary, Clive, it's stopped raining", called their mother.

They all rushed downstairs, nearly tripping over each other in excitement. "How about taking Paddy for a walk in the Black Forest?" Mrs. Wilson asked. "We'd love to!" shouted all four children together.

Just as they were going out of the gate, the postman arrived with a little parcel for Mary. It was from their aunt. You see it was her birthday that day. They all rushed back into the house. Mary tore off the paper as fast as she could. Inside the parcel was a little watch, with a gold strap.

Chapter Two
The Black Forest

Mary put on her new watch and they set off once again. The forest was not far off, so they did not have to hurry. Usually when they went into the forest they walked on the wide path so that they would not be able to get lost. "Today let's go a different way", said John. "All right", agreed the others.

After a while it began to get dark, so they turned to go home, when all of a sudden Elizabeth gave a cry. "This isn't the way we came!" she said. "I don't recognise this path at all!" "Nor me," said Chris. "Well I don't either so that must mean we have taken the wrong path."

"O dear", said Mary and she began to cry. "Never mind", comforted Elizabeth "We'll soon find our way home again".

Chapter Three
Lost

They went on and on but they just could not find the right path home again.

At last they came to a little cave in a rock, where John said that they had better stay for the night. That morning they were just waking themselves up, when Clive rolled over, then suddenly he disappeared. The others were so surprised they could not speak. John was the first one to speak. "Where did he go?"

"I don't know." said Elizabeth.

Mary went to see, then she disappeared too. "Oh I know!" said John "there must be a hole somewhere over there".

Chapter Four
The Secret Passage

They went to see and sure enough there was quite a big hole. They both climbed through and found themselves in a long dark passage.

Luckily John had his torch in his pocket, so they were able to see the way. The further they went the darker it grew, and they could never see the end. They all wondered how long it was going to be until the end, or what time it was.

Eventually they saw a little cave with little chairs carved out of the wall. They went to look at it when suddenly two men sprang up on them.

PTO

Chapter Five
Captured

"Gosh!" said John to the others. "I've never had such a shock in all my life". "It gave me a fright too," said Mary. "I wonder who those men were." "Yes, and I wonder how we're going to get out of here!" said Elizabeth. "That's exactly what I was thinking," said Clive.

"Listen," said John "I've been thinking and I've thought of a plan to help us escape". "What?" cried the others, all at once. "Well you see we could all pretend that we were feeling sick, then the men would come and let us out, because they would not want us to be sick all over their beautiful prison." The others laughed. "When they let us out, I will trip them up, and we can get a good start while they are looking for their canteen." "Oh" interrupted Mary "what's that thing over there?" They all rolled over to it. They picked up the 'thing' as Mary had put it.

It was a shiny emerald. " We must keep this", he said and put it in his pocket.

Chapter Six.
Escaped

Now, to get back to escaping. John said "let's start now!" "Alright" said the others. "I'm ready" said Clive, and off they went. Everybody walked, and when they had escaped, they started to concentrate on getting out of the cave. At least they found their way out. "Oh!" said Elizabeth. "I have just remembered I've got my compass in my pocket." "Just like girls!" said John.

They soon found their way home, and was their mother pleased to see them again!

Chapter Seven
Back Home Again

They told their mother all about their adventures, when all of a
sudden, John remembered the emerald in his pocket. He took it
out and showed it to his mother. "Oh" she said. "This is called
'The Emerald of The Country'. The police have been looking for
it everywhere." She continued "You have solved a great
mystery. I think you will get a reward."

They did, and the reward was forty pounds. They shared it
out between them and had ten pounds each, but they always
remembered to walk on the wide path in future.

THE END

Introduction

This story is about Pam and Julie./ ~~Mackinoy~~ ~~who~~ ~~live~~ ~~in~~ ~~Scotland~~. One day they discover a battered, old boat shed and inside they find a rowing boat named 'Seabird'. They decide to keep it as nobody seems to own it. Julie who is ten, but five minutes older than her twin Pam, decides that it would be more exciting to go for their first ride in it at night. So they creep out one night and after rowing for about fifteen minutes, they find a little island hidden by rocks and rushes. Lots of mysterious happenings appear after that, but I will leave you to find out what.

Chapter 1
The Boat Shed

"Julie! Where are you?" shouted Pam for the third time.
"Here, in the cloakroom", Julie replied. Pam ran into the
cloakroom and found her twin putting on her coat and hat.
    "I'm going for a walk on the moors. Coming?"
    "Alright. I'm just going to fetch my earmuffs".
    They were soon walking briskly along on the deserted
moors. It was early morning and the wind stung their faces
as the twins strode along. They soon came to the most
lonely part of the moors, where hardly anybody ever went.
This part was covered with heather which looked like a
blanket from above.
    "We've never been here before have we?" Julie asked.
"Mmmm" said Julie thoughtfully. Pam however interrupted
her thoughts by pointing to a little hut.
    "What on earth is that doing here?" she demanded.
    "Let's go and see", said Julie simply. She was already
running towards it, so Pam followed. As they came closer,
they saw that it was not a hut at all, but a tiny boat shed.
"Let's go and see what's inside", Pam said eagerly. They ran
round the shed but found no door. "How very peculiar!"
exclaimed Julie, mystified. "Look there's a tiny window here.
Maybe we could get in there, came Pam's voice from the
other side of the shed. Julie rounded the shed and found
Pam peeping through a little window with no glass in it.

Chapter 2
Sea Bird

 "It's creepy in here" came Pam's voice. "What's that?" She
froze in fright.
    "it's only the echo of your voice, silly," taught Julie.
    After a few difficulties the twins managed to squeeze
through the little window.
    "Have you got a torch Julie?" inquired Pam, for it was pitch
black within the wooden walls of the mysterious little building.

"Sorry, but I didn't know we would have to use a torch in the daylight, so I didn't bring mine," Julie replied regretfully.

"Oh well, we'll have to do without it."

Their eyes soon got used to the light and, going to explore the other side of the side of the shed Pam tripped and fell.

"You clumsy thing!" said Julie scornfully. She ran to help her twin up. Pam struggled to her feet, and looked down to see what she had tripped over. To her amazement she saw a rough hole cut in the ground, with a rowing boat fitted in it.

"Look in that hole, it has something inside it." It looked very strange so Julie felt as though she was entitled to whisper.

Without further hesitation Julie lifted Pam up, and Pam reached to grab the key from the hook she saw above her.

"It seems very peculiar to lock a trapdoor and leave the key where it can easily be found," remarked Julie, voicing Pam's thoughts.

However they soon had the rusty old key in the lock.

"It's jolly stiff," Pam panted after a while.

At last, after a lot of pulling and tugging they managed to open the stubborn old trapdoor. Yet another surprise met their bewildered eyes. It was a long dark passage.

"Let's come back here later on and we can explore then," decided Julie at last. "It's getting late and if we don't get back we'll miss breakfast.

Chapter 3
Adventure In The Dark

That day the twins had to run errands for their mother and the only spare moment they received was interrupted by visitors.

That evening they decided they would wait no longer and once in bed, Pam whispered to Julie who was in the opposite bed, "Pssst, Julie, what about going to explore tonight at midnight? It would be much more exciting."

"Good idea," Julie whispered back, "I'll set my alarm clock for midnight and put it under my pillow. No-one will be able to hear it except me".

Julie crept out of bed and over to her dressing table. She fumbled about for the alarm clock

On her way she tripped over the waste paper basket and it fell to the floor with a crash! All the odds and ends scattered themselves on the floor. Julie fled back to bed ,like a frightened mouse.

Fortunately their mother was on the telephone, so she could not come and investigate that minute, and by the time she did, they had collected the rubbish and put them into the waste paper bin, which they had put back into place. Having done this they leapt back into their beds and pretended to be asleep.

"It must have been my imagination," their mother said softly, after she had heard their peaceful snores.

At last Julie was awakened by her alarm clock. It rang out, rather muffled, in Julie's ear. She sat up and yawned. After moving the alarm clock from under her pillow, she put it back on the dressing table. Having done this, she moved silently towards Pam, who was snoring. She gave her a little shake and Pam awoke with a start.

"What's the matter? Do you have to wake me at this time of night?" Pam said crossly. Julie looked a bit taken aback.

"It's midnight silly, we're going exploring," her twin replied impatiently.

"Oh, of course, I forgot." Pam said, jumping out of bed.

They quickly dressed themselves in slacks, thick pullovers and scarves. Then they picked up their heavy shoes and tip-toed downstairs. They did not put on their shoes until they reached the front door. As soon as they reached it they slipped on their shoes and Pam quietly unlocked the door. Once outside she locked the door again and slipped the key into her pocket, and they set off across the moors at a brisk pace.

It was a long walk, and by the time the twins reached the hut it was ten minutes to one a.m. They climbed in at the window as usual, but as Pam reached for the key, Julie gave a start. "Pam, Pam, there's no key here!"

Chapter 4
No Key To The Mystery

Pam trembled. "But I'm sure we put the key back here", she whispered.

"We did. I can remember you putting it back after I had said we would miss our breakfast", Julie said, after having racked her memory.

She shone the torch up to the hook, to make sure it was empty, and it was. She then pulled thoughtlessly at the trapdoor, and to her surprise it moved slightly. She pulled again and it moved a crack.

"Pam, I'm sure we did close that door. But if we did, how can the key jump down from the hook and unlock the trapdoor all by itself? Because that what it appears to have done."

"Don't be silly, Julie. You know very well it couldn't have done that," Pam scolded.

"Well where is it then?" Julie demanded losing her temper.

"Don't ask me!" Pam said, getting cross.

All this time the trapdoor had slowly been opening. Now, the deep, dark hole yawned beneath the arguing twins.

Chapter 5
A Very Strange Fact

The twins stopped arguing once they saw the dark hole. "It's a good thing we brought torches," Pam remarked. "No," said Julie, who had not been listening to what Pam had said. Before Pam could speak, she added, "How are we going to get down there anyway?" "That's a thought," agreed Pam thoughtfully, "But there's probably a rope ladder or something." Sure enough there was. "But Julie, I've just thought of something. Where's the boat?" she added, in a terrified whisper. " Someone's been here before us, and they've unlocked the trapdoor with that key and kept it. "They've probably taken the boat as well," Julie said.

"But how could anyone get a boat down there?" inquired Pam, lying on her stomach and peeping over the edge of the hole.

"Oh I don't know, but come on, or else we won't have any time to explore." She started climbing down the ladder. Pam followed.

"This ladder seems to go on for ever," Julie complained after ten minutes solid descending. "My legs are aching". She shone her torch down to see how much further they had to go. Not much further. Only about five yards. She looked up at Pam. Then suddenly, as if remembering what she had seen she looked down again. "Pam!" she gasped

Chapter 6
The Strange Encounter

Pam looked and when she saw what Pam had seen a shiver went down her spine and she began to wish she was back in bed, so that she could feel cosy and safe. Then she found Pam's body snuggled up next to her. Her hand felt very warm when she tried to squeeze it with her cold one. She whispered gently in Julie's ear. "Was it just a dream? Are you still climbing down that ladder?" She was very confused. But Julie just went on snoring..

A FIGURE WAS LURKING

Pam decided unhappily that she would have to wait till the morning, or else Julie might get very cross about waking up in the middle of the night. She could not go back to sleep though, because she was still a bit scared about what might be waiting for her in her dream. But she was very glad that Julie was in the same bed next to her, even though she was snoring loudly.

In the morning she woke up again. She knew that she must have been asleep. But she dared not say anything about what might have happened because she thought that Julie would just laugh at her. So she just tried to act normally. But Julie did wake up when she felt Pam's cold hand and shouted, "What are you doing in my bed?" Pam felt silly and replied guiltily, "I don't know. I'm only trying to warm up."

They were both very glad that now it was time for breakfast.

THE END

The Cruel Sea

Cruel, cruel are the Seven Seas,
When in anger do they kill;
Ships are received into eerie depths
And once-active limbs lie still.

Down, down in the Ocean's depths
Bones and skulls lie strewn,
Existing in a phantom silence
In the Ocean's guilty tomb.

The sight of a simple wooden frame
Being tossed from billow to billow's crest;
Then ruthlessly torn apart and thrown
To its final place of eternal rest.

Cruel, cruel are the Seven Seas —
Cruel to the Innocent life
That sails in fear on the Ocean's wave
Aware of the terror of eternal strife.

USES OF MAIZE

1. CORN OIL

2. STARCH

3. CORNFLOUR

4. CATTLE FODDER

5. POPCORN

6. CORN FLAKES

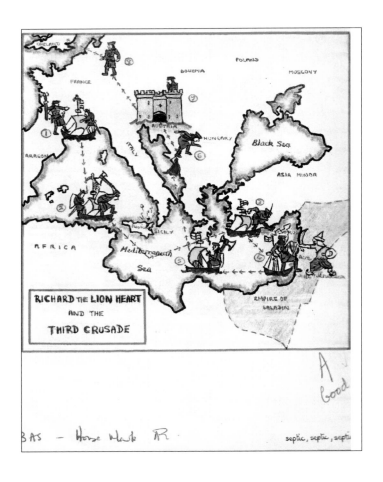

RICHARD THE **LION HEART**
AND THE
THIRD CRUSADE

BAS - Horse Work R.

septic, septic, septi

A
Good

A MEDIEVAL VILLAGE

ENGLISH LONG-BOW MAN ABOUT 1300

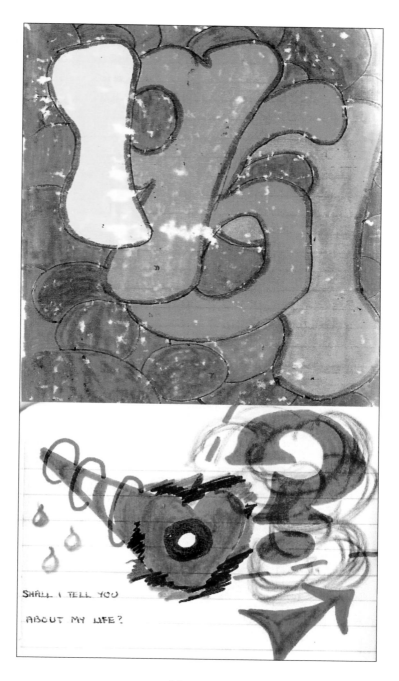

The sun is up
The sky is blue
It's beautiful
And so are you.

In bed at the moment — that's
why my writing's funny.

Friday Jan 17th

Daddy's just walked in and insulted me by asking if this was where 'the noise' was coming from, when I was singing 'Dear Prudence'.

Had a ghastly dream last night – I was eating chicken and there was a long white thing like a nerve in it. I cut it out and it was still attached to bits of chicken, then it lifted it's head up and started swaying it about. It was a horrible tapeworm. Why've we got to learn about such ghastly things in Biology? I'm going through a dream phase at the moment.

Sunday Jan 19th

Spent about 2 hrs. this morning going through all the stages of eating a jaffa orange with great care and attention to the senses while eating. Wrote down results. All that lunacity to 'describe in v. great detail a Jaffa orange' for the English essay. Turned out two and a bit sides!!!

Tuesday Jan 21st

Dreamt of Gerry last night - funny that – I'm sure I'm not mad on him anymore. Everyone was at the crossing and they were all pretending not to know him. I grinned and he grinned back and I followed him into W.H. Smiths. He was looking at the books and I was coming round the middle shelves towards him. Very sweet except that was when I woke up – would be.

Wednesday Jan 29th

I'm completely cracked today. Terrible
happenings after Life Class yesterday
evening. Sue got blown up by Mr.
Blenkinsop because she left her purse in the
formroom. The cleaner refused to clean it as
she thought if it was pinched she'd be
accused. Sue defended herself – Mr. B.
accused her of being cheeky, Sue burst into
tears.
Went bell-ringing –great! Mick's a loony –
terribly funny, I tried to set the bell, failed,
everything went haywire and I banged my
head against the wall. Mick dashed over
and said, "you all right – sure? – Let's see
your hands" Examined them minutely,
eventually satisfied.
While Sally was ringing he said to her
"Don't keep trying to hold my hand – I
know you like it but don't!." He's round the
twist.

Wednesday Feb 5th

I've come to the decision, at last, after three years, that Kathleen and Carolyn should be best friends. They go well together, and I don't much care any more. Trouble is they always go silly and stupid as they have an effect on each other.

Read the most horrible story in '19' yesterday about a slightly mental girl who had a 'thing' about mirrors.

WHo are they?

Is she me?

SUN. FEB. 16

Arrived at Fiona's about 8.15. Sallie got off with a zombie-like creature. Deaky got off with Fiona's brother. Sally and I had the most hysterical time out. We were advanced upon by five weeds. Before that this creature came up to me and said, "If you're not with anyone, how about coming over here and participating"!

Shook him off only to be asked by another weed. V. bravely refused. Joined Sally dancing when these other five weeds creatures started closing in. As soon as the record finished we dashed outside and were followed by the long lanky beanpole who had made a succession of grabs at Deaky (she'd escaped). He then proceeded to put his arm around my waist. Shook him off and we dashed back in again. The other four had closed in again and one started the "My name's...what's yours?" lark. By that time we were both in absolute fits of laughter but it didn't seem to discourage them. The 'name' one, Tony, then asked me if I wanted a drink. As I did, I said yes and we went over to get one. Sally came over then with one of the other creatures who'd asked her the same question, adding an arm at the bargain. She said "I asked for a drink that's all"!!! We finished the drinks and came back near the fire.

Tony then wanted a smooth dance, but I said, "No thank you, I'm too cold" Didn't make sense - I think he thought I was crazy. Worked anyway. We made another escape later - went and talked to Leslie - she's awfully nice. Followed out again - this time they wanted to take us home.. They went at last, but then of course this other creature who'd been trying hard to get off with some-one all evening came and asked me to dance. Said no again. By this time I was thoroughly cold and rather miserable, seeing everyone else having a good time.

Anyway I suppose it was rather entertaining but really I've never seen such a lot of weeds in one place, in all my life.

Friday July 25th

All's a haze. Odd's life. Covered in a cloudy shroud – is that what's nearest, that a dream long ago, may be a reality, but uncared for? A distance away, yet nearer by far than mere 'few miles'? What is distance? An object, an obstacle that does not exist, but is there, chased through life forever? Or so it seems. What's the point, the point that cannot be helped, a dream lasting a few days. But reality returns and hems me in. Isolated on a cloud, watches the progress of others. Advises without experience, as it would feel the reason for separation. Division. Without sense. Water forever. A floor and always another. The future?????????

Contentment cannot be defined. A few words can cheer. A stimulant – like food one can starve without replenishment. And so it is. To benefit while completion is impossible. Yet otherwise to be nothing.

COLOURS

When your face
appeared over my crumpled life
at first I understood
only the poverty of what I have.
Then it's particular light
on woods, on rivers, on the sea,
became my beginning in the coloured world
in which I had not yet had my beginning.
I am so frightened, I am so frightened
of the unexpected sunrise finishing,
of revelations
and tears and the excitement finishing.
I don't fight it, my love is this fear.
I nourish it, who can nourish nothing,
love's slipshod watchman.
Fear hems me in.
I am conscious that these minutes are short
and that the colours in my eyes will vanish
when your face sets. GS 1969

GS 1969

GS 1969

45

GS 1971

GS 1971

COUNCIL FOR
NATIONAL ACADEMIC AWARDS

GILLIAN KATHRYN SHAW

has been awarded the degree of

BATCHELOR OF ARTS

with First Class Honours having completed
a full-time course in

GRAPHIC DESIGN

at BRISTOL POLYTECHNIC in 1976

SCHOOL OF GRAPHIC ARTS
DEPARTMENT OF GRAPHIC INFORMATION
ROYAL COLLEGE OF ART

Degree Show 1978

GILLIAN SHAW
Born in London 1954
Bristol Polytechnic 1973-76
BA in Graphic Design 1978

Awarded a Gulbenkian grant for joint production
of educational material about young homeless people in cities

Information needs designing

We are a graphic design partnership specialising in the design of information. We have a strong ergonomic approach to design – we analyse the problem carefully and design a solution that is tailored to the needs of the people who will eventually use it. We often do this simply by talking to people to find out what they would find useful and we monitor our ideas by information testing at an early stage of design.

The service we offer is based on the belief that in the communication of facts and ideas, language should be as important a consideration to the designer as presentation. By integrating these two areas, we aim to make information easier to understand and easier to use.

Bill Mayblin MA(RCA)   Gillian Shaw MA(RCA)

Mayblin/Shaw Information design
Caledonian Road
London N1 9DN

In those days
we worked
with rulers,
Letterex, light
boxes, pens,
pencils,
tracing paper
and lots more
time!
The computer
had barely
been created.

An account by a colleague in 1982
When Gill Became Ill

We met through working together. I don't think either of us
expected to become close friends. It was in 1980 and I had taken
on the job of producing a touring photographic exhibition about
El Salvador for the work 'Camerawork' and the El Salvador
Solidarity Campaign. I had assumed there would be photographs
easily available, but there were only a few reproductions of
mutilated bodies.

So I had to start from the beginning, with photographs from
America and from French photo-journalists.

The project had become enormously delayed and I was very
concerned that we would never finish it. My colleagues had no
experience of producing exhibitions and we were all struggling.
We were committed to the idea of producing work which could
be used as soon as possible for campaigning and there were all
sorts of tensions between us. I knew we needed someone to use
their graphic skills to help me relax with my images and text.
'Graphic Design Workshop' was recommended to me, where I
met Gill, one of the partners. I was surprised when they said
that their company would help me and was scared they would
change their minds once they realised how much work the
exhibition would need. But in fact Gill became just as involved
and dedicated to the project as we were.

It's hard to remember Gill as she was then. I've known her
longer since she's been ill and undoubtedly our friendship must
have altered by what's happened. She seemed much tougher
than most women I knew. I admired her style in either making
her design ideas work, or discarding them immediately. She
seemed to have it all worked out somehow – her personal style,
her mini and her house. She always wore red and green clothes.
She was the only woman I knew who did not wear jeans all the
time. She always looked immaculate, and I was dazzled by her
ability to look casual in her graphic design style .

Gill became the centre of our group very quickly and made
it change. Suddenly it all revolved around Gill. We needed
her to make us work much more quickly and became her

slaves in answering her questions and providing her with food and drink. I resented that at first, but somehow realised we needed it to get things finished quickly.

Working on the exhibition was very intense. We believed we were doing something important to influence people in seeing the population of El Salvador as real people, rather than backward, nameless peasants.

We lived together, worked together and thought of little else. At the end of one of those exhausting days, we were both focused on one of the photographs I'd been working with. It was of a row of soldiers standing behind a row of corpses in tattered civilian clothes. One of the soldiers had a sword in his hand, which he'd been using to amputate one of the civilian's legs. It was a horrific picture and I've no idea how the photographer had been able to take it. We both started crying and were devastated at how we all had become immune to all that horror and cruelty that must have still been going on there.

After we'd completed that exhibition, we continued working together, but didn't see each other so regularly.

When Gill caught flu, I phoned her every day, because I was worried about her being on her own, although she insisted that her colleagues were looking after her. Because she seemed to be getting better, I did not bother to ring her one day. The following morning, when I was alone in my office, the phone rang. It was one of her friends from work, to tell me that he'd phoned her yesterday and when he'd had no reply, had been round to see her to see if she was alright. He'd found her unconscious. She was taken into hospital and started having fits.

Seeing Gill in hospital then was one of the worst times of my life. It is a jumbled mixtures of memories now and it's difficult to put them in any order. She didn't know who I was. That was the first shock. I knew she was feeling embarrassed about not recognising me and I felt so helpless. The first time she talked to me she had no idea about where she was, or about what had happened. She was anxious for me to explain, but she did not seem able to take anything in. She kept asking the same questions every few minutes.

Her memory was damaged and she was so weak and vulnerable, but nothing anyone said seemed to affect her, because she seemed unable to digest it.

All her friends and family started visiting her and her condition varied every day. We would think she was improving, then she'd get worse.

One day I went to see her with another of her friends, feeling fairly cheerful, because she had seemed alright the day before. But we found her bed empty and suddenly thought she might be dead. She'd been moved into a different place, where her body was surrounded by screens. She was lying unconscious with a drip up her nose. We fled back down that corridor, blundering, hand in hand to find the exit as soon as we could.

We found out later that she had nearly died, but that she was still alive now. Because she only remembered certain people, I think most of us felt that we wanted to be with her and work with her to bring back those bits of missing memory. She remembered my name, but nothing about our friendship. She never remembered those months from just before her illness.

So, in a way, the first Gill I knew had disappeared from both our minds. Our friendship now is post-illness, which makes trying to see the changes very difficult. She's much softer, but otherwise very much the same person, although we don't have a working relationship anymore. The sort of professional design she once had is the last thing she's interested in. It's very easy sometimes to ignore what Gill's illness has meant, because of her attitude to it. She never complains or gives up the struggle to overcome her disability.

MY Mother's Memory

It was May 1982. We were living in
Luxembourg and had just got back from a
holiday in Corfu when we received a
telephone call from my sister telling us
that Gillian was seriously ill in hospital. I
flew back to London next morning and I
shall never forget her face when she saw
me. She burst into tears and sobbed for a
good fifteen minutes. When I was concerned
and looked up at the nurse, I was told it
was the best thing. Having lost memory,
she could not understand where she was or
what was happening.

From that day I stayed at the hospital and
had to leave notes when I had to go to have a
meal, as she would not remember and know that I

would return. She was a child again, holding onto my hand for confidence

After six weeks, when her strength returned, she came back to live with us in Luxembourg. We returned to London in August for a check-up with her consultant and that day in the surgery she announced, completely to my surprise, that she wanted to go back to her own home and get her independence back. Her strength of character appeared as early as that, when she was still having very severe seizures. It was very hard for me to let her do that, because although she thought she would cope, she really had become a very young girl, who had no memory and had to learn the basic activities of cooking and looking after herself..

HERE I AM AGAIN...

Still A Child in November 1982

I need to talk to someone about the changes that have happened to my mind and body. These changes in myself are very strong and today they have come to the surface and appear as if they might be very relevant to this illness I have. I feel I should explore them and try to understand more, rather than just drift along passively. But who should I consult for information? I am worried, but I do not know who to consult. I am frightened about showing any emotion.

I have never spent so much time doing nothing at all, allowing my brain to be so unoccupied like this. I am allowing myself to lie about, lazy, with no conscience whatsoever. My nothingness has improved slightly though, by viewing myself as a child, who has to be taught how to live. I feel now that maybe everything: the fits, the loss of memory, and my new self, may be in a knot somewhere in my brain.

I should try and understand more, but I do not know where to start.

My family had to let me go,
even when their hearts said "NO!"

My mother, my father and my sister had all
been looking after me so well, but I insisted on
searching for my independence.

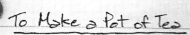

To Make a Pot of Tea

1. Fill up the kettle with water and don't forget to turn on the electricity or the water will probably turn itself off!

2. Find mugs somewhere in the top cupboard over the kettle. The spoons should be in the drawer underneath the kettle.

3. Get the milk out of the fridge while waiting for the water to boil.

4. Then pour a bit of boiling water into the tea pot if you are using one and swirl it around so that you heat up the pot.

5. ~~Pour a bit~~ Find the tea bags (they should be near the mugs in a cupboard in a cardboard box) Put in as many as you think you'll need – usually there's no need than 1 for 2 people but sometimes they want it stronger. It may be worth asking them!

6. Cover tea bags with water. Don't forget that some people will want more than one mug. Stir in the tea before leaving it to brew and cover up the pot to keep it warm if you can find a cover.

Good luck

FRUSTRATION (1985)

Dear friends,

I feel handicapped because none of you are really sharing my problem, but I understand that you are prepared to help me as much as you are able to.

The handicap means that sometimes I wake up in the morning to find one of the switches in my brain has not been switched on for no particular reason. So I remain fuzzy for the rest of the day and my intelligence doesn't operate. It is very frustrating for me and I realise that it's frustrating for you too, the way it manifests itself in my stupidity. But you must accept it. It is a disability and I have no control of it. Some of you don't seem to understand what it means and how it affects me. So without being too much of a bore, let me remind you of the main effect.

Whatever my mood, if I have a fit, it will empty my brain and I could wake up with all last night's switches alight, or at least with the dimmer on. But the light remains dull and there is nothing I can do to change that wretched bulb again. It is the most frustrating thing I have ever experienced and gets more frustrating as I get better, because the more I recognise it, the further it is from my control.

I want you all to try very hard not to make me feel stupid, because it takes all the strength I've got left to keep my self-confidence reasonably intact. So when you get frustrated with me, please remember that I'm probably feeling just as frustrated with myself.

Also, I want you to try and understand my learning disabilities. They do exist. My brain appears to have been cleaned out, so that in order to clarify some of the rather dull shapes in there, I have to go over those lines again and again, which makes me feel very embarrassed. Sometimes I sense you thinking, "Oh no, not again. She must know by now!" I need more encouragement from you all in order to improve. Please be patient.

.   From   Gill

Living With A Fit in April 1986

I came back early during the day, knowing I could do with some sleep. One hour later, I woke in the grip of one of the most torturing fits I knew of. Even while it was going on, I was aware enough to tell myself I must remember it all. I must make notes before it slipped away. It seemed important because I was aware of my body and feelings at that moment, even though the physical dynamics of my limbs were completely beyond my control. I was desperately trying to restrain the shaking of my right arm, but the shakes were beyond my comprehension. Yet I could feel them cutting, like millions of tiny, excruciating sharp knives into my feeling.

I could hear myself just managing to put together the words "I can't bear it!" It was so exhausting, that even while it went on, I knew it was going to shatter me. I would do better to black out completely, if only I knew how!

This went on for about three minutes. Even then it just withdrew slowly, so that my awareness merely hobbled after it. I was given no break. What an experience that was!

Afterwards, I lay flat on my bed, with my eyes open, staring at the ceiling and probably with my mouth wide open too. I had no thought of any dignity. I had no drop of energy left in any remote recess of my body. But about thirty minutes later my phone rang and I found myself picking up the receiver with new hands and speaking normally, with what appeared to be a new voice.

62

SOME THOUGHTS

Some thoughts provide some kind of sign!
Those flimsy thoughts may still be mine!
Now good thoughts may be there somewhere,
to build new ones no longer bare.
Tangled up in some messy strife,
they still emerge with some reason for life.
I must try writing them down somewhere
to find a language I'm happy to share.

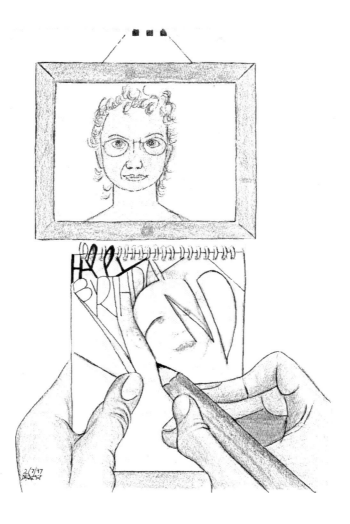

Yesterday

I have found a drawing from my past to say
that yesterday wasn't as good as today.
When told that my brain was to be ill forever
it was not too easy to feel bright or clever.
To speak thoughts, to talk, to find the right words.
In this miserable place nothing happy was heard.
Whilst uprooting weeds to leave space for flowers,
what was worthwhile to provide me with powers?
I had to remember, not just to forget;
I had to believe that some help could be met.

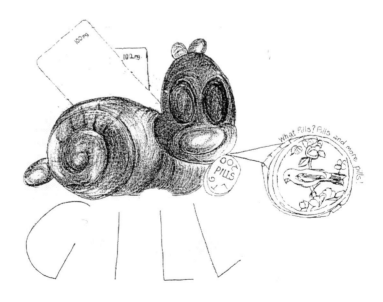

Today

There should be no reason to feel grey today
after all those good feelings I felt yesterday.
I hear nothing but swirling wet wind even so.
Strong rain just batters against the window.
Garden colours have lost all their smiles,
overgrown by weeds and piles of old tiles.
Memories awake, just feeble and bare.
I must have forgotten, tomorrow is there.

Now then

Being well may seem as faint as a star,
when my past seems lost and so very far.
But some strength to live in the here and now
is there to find something real anyhow.
I can open some doors and climb out of my past
with belief that some real good will surely last.
I may not find all that I want right now,
but I will start my real progress anyhow.
I may have to walk up some unlikely paths
and enjoy being soothed in some very hot baths.
But now with a true faith in Jesus being here,
I will wait in bad times for good things to appear.

Different Seizures in January 1990

I came back to reality from all the rubbish, with great
excitement about believing I was getting better about
'controlling' my fits. But the word 'control' is the wrong one.
I have used it for many years without questioning what I really
mean. I should say 'accept' or 'acknowledge' or 'live with'. I
have not achieved enough control over my fits, although, as I
get better, they seem to allow my brain to move back into
place.

They used to terrify me, because I was unable to recognise
anything for some time after I regained consciousness. Being in
that state used to last for hours, but nowadays only for a few
minutes. I'm far less likely to panic now, although I still
appreciate reassurance from someone calming me by holding
my hand. If they can't do that, they can always help me by just
using a few simple words to explain what has just happened to
me. Then my brain can relax and start to work again, when I
am able to recognise what has happened.

A friend related to me once about taking me out during the
early days of my illness, when neither of us knew much about
fits. He told me how I had had a fit while we were eating
together in a restaurant. He described how he had nearly
suffocated me by trying to stop my strange movements.
People at other tables appeared to be shocked, by what
appeared to them to be some kind of passionate embrace.
They probably had never seen any epilepsy before, so were
unable to accept any explanation from us.

I sometimes have fits without any warning at all. They can be
difficult to recognise, regardless of all my previous
experiences. I usually feel as though I'm about to get a very
bad cold and everything seems very hazy. Everything I
encounter seems worthless. Sometimes I am confronted by fits
in dangerous places and people often ask me why I can't be
more careful. But I can't always be so astute and I want to get
on with my life.

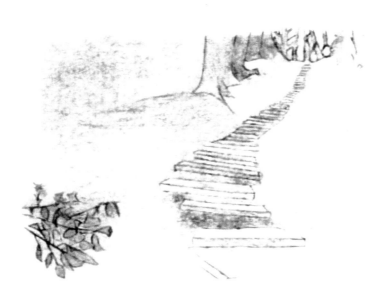

Good Old Epilepsy in February 1992

At last I have started writing in my diary again after leaving it empty for a month. The last few days have been rather strange because I have been feeling very tired, but able to watch myself wanting to come alive again. I've had no real fits, just a few jerks here and there and I am beginning to think perhaps I need a good old fit to get me out of this moronic state. At least I can talk to people about it. I am beginning to think this is my new state of living, in up and down moods all the time.

I woke up a few days ago in a very aggressive state and started attacking people I recognised with any words I could find on any subject. They just thought I was in a bad mood. I nattered on about anything that was on my mind.

Learning To Relax in June 1997

I tired myself out by doing more than usual, having no rest, but still cooking a casserole for the friends I was expecting later. I went to bed later than usual that night because I had been enjoying myself. When I started getting ready for bed, everything disappeared.

I woke feeling very unhappy, realising I was about to have a fit. I could feel my muscles tensing and could feel no strength to overpower them. I knew all my limbs were trying to jerk about, but I would not let them. I knew there was help somewhere, but I was very confused. I was grabbing for support and at the same time for air to breathe.

Then I heard a soft, calming voice, even though all I could perceive was a huge wet bunch of mushrooms swamping me. I was stuck in mud, in great pain and feeling minute and hopeless.

I must have been growing more savage, because I knew I was having some kind of nightmare. Something tried to reassure me and I tried to sweep every bad thought from my brain. I had lost every string of confidence.

I had to realise I was growing more and more tiny and believed I was about to snap. The more flimsy I became, the larger the mushrooms grew. I tried to protect myself from them by smashing everything in sight. I believed if I gave up, everything would disappear forever. I was terrified.

Then at last I noticed a faint spot of light which I could just feel strength enough to grab. But I collapsed, not caring anymore what was going to happen. I could hear a comforting voice near me and believed I could just let someone else get on with me. But I had no voice to speak and remained that way for some time. The jerks seemed to diminish and I became calm enough to go to sleep at last.

images and

I can think thoughts with images many times
and they become stronger with tangible rhymes.
Words and images share meaning between them
and will come alive when I try to retrieve them.
Important thoughts will not let me sleep.
They show up in the most unlikely heap.
Strong images trusted to give their support
can be seen now I know I do want to be taught.
In my past there may have been little to say,
but now there is little to find in the way.

A Good Fit in November 1997

I was sitting down to relax because I had started feeling unusually hot. My brain told me I had better be careful, so I headed for the living room. I managed to grab a piece of paper and a pencil on the way, so that I would be able to scribble some notes to use later.

I noticed bruised feelings in my eyes. I thought this could be because I was feeling tired, so I told myself to slow down. I felt a heavy feeling in my chest and my cheeks started twitching, then my arms, then my shoulders. My fingers started jerking too.

I knew I should take myself seriously and relax somewhere as soon as possible. But I was worried that if I relaxed, a fit would overcome me. I could see a monster waiting for an opportunity to grab hold of me. I wanted to find every bit of energy inside me to fight it. My chest seemed to work the hardest to keep me awake. It would not allow me to be bound up in any ghastly knot.

It was very hard to keep balanced enough to keep notes, but I had to try very hard or I would get pains in my chest. Then, if I let go, I would just disintegrate into nothing.

I had to relax a bit, because I just told myself I must. I started seeing flashes of vague pictures. I wanted to close my eyes, but I could not let go. I was being supported somehow.

I noticed every sound becoming louder, as though my hearing had taken over my brain, or at least had become helpful. My stomach muscles appeared then, jerking gently, as though they wanted to help. They made me feel stronger. I thought I may be able to dash about inside my body and check everything.

I could close my eyes. I noticed every muscle was very vulnerable, but at least I could smile again.

Starting To Understand in August 1998

I was reading what I had written a few weeks ago, just before breaking my ankle. I was very interested in the fit I had then. I could see how similar it was to the one I'd had whilst my ankle was recovering. The plaster had been removed and I was slowly becoming used to my muscles again.

I noticed how the strength I needed to use my leg was linked to my fits. The muscles in both my mind and my body must be very close. I had not realised this until I had to live with this broken ankle, although I had always suspected it. That must be something to do with why I can usually improve my fits. I am convinced that those two parts of me must be linked with each other, whenever I could let them be.

That was why I was able to improve my ankle relatively fast, able to walk about slowly, without needing any support anymore, even though I had needed crutches at first, whilst I had plaster around my ankle.

When the plaster had gone, I still had to have some fits. But they were not any worse than the ones I was used to. Some of them were the type that I had managed to control, but a few of them knocked me out completely.

Then, one week ago, stress must have been building up. I had been doing things I was not used to. Everything combined into one very bad fit. It was worse than usual because I could not let go of the very tight elastic bands that appeared to be stretching furiously in my brain. I seemed to be part of a swamping blackness, which I believed would dissolve into nothing at all. There was no alternative for me than to be part of it.

I connected this state with my idea of dying. After all, I had recently broken my ankle, so there was no surprise that I was feeling so bad.

Although the last few fits had not been as bad, they seemed to have been building up together into this terrible one.

I believed I needed to find help desperately, but I had no idea where to find any.

Peace in July 1999

I woke up at two in the morning, after having a fit that had been much longer than usual those days. At least I felt part of it instead of feeling destroyed by it. This time I felt it was time to stop.

I was being watched by some group of beings, who were supposed to be assessing the situation, but did not really know any answers.

My main worry was about loneliness for the future. All the carers had disappeared, so I was left stranded, with absolutely nothing.

I did not panic though, because I found that my brain was still working, and maybe my senses. They were sending me to find some clean sheets to deal with my wet bed. I was sensible enough to go downstairs and make myself something to drink, to relax with on the sofa. I believed I was being intelligent enough to bring some other part of myself to life.

I could not concentrate on any detail. I could not focus on any letters, but I managed to be stimulated by some pictures. Something must have been alive, because I was still happy enough to look. I decided to find some peaceful music to go to sleep with.

I must be asleep, now that nothing makes sense.
My home seems so dark. Even so, I'm less tense.
I have to leave some memory tied up in sockets.
The rest may not want to climb out of my pockets.
Never mind, lovely water lilles still float away
when the fishermen seem to have something at bay!
There's lots to acknowledge in my past anyway
Now that I hold most of my fits well at bay.

75

Ask, and you will receive; seek and you will find;
knock, and the door will be opened to you.
For everyone who asks will receive, and he who seeks will find,
and the door will be opened to anyone who knocks.
(Luke 9 v10-11)

Happiness in my home

1st June 1998 Gillian Shaw's Place

My Garden in Rusthall

New Life with Ken

*We brought new life
into each other
throughout the years
we loved each other.*

I taught Ken to cook and Ken taught me to walk.

Ken died peacefully in 2002

YOGA

I've been using Yoga classes for many years, to help me find co-ordination, strength, and balance in times of stress.

I've been able to encourage my muscles to work automatically, instead of allowing them to turn off in the midst of bad fits.

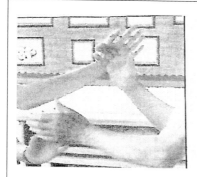 

Weekly Tai Chi classes make me work hard
in looking for harmony between my mind
and my body, in pace with everyone else in the class.
It is very challenging, very energetic
and demands a lot of concentration,
which provides good exercise for my brain
as well as my limbs!

Night-time Memories in 2002

One evening I made myself extra tired and had no trouble falling asleep that night. I seemed to wake up in the middle of the night in front of my computer screen. It seemed to be talking to me. The words on the screen made sense and they appeared, without me having to use my fingers to write them.

They created a story which grew out of my past. I did not want to remember it, but I knew I had been rescued from something.

There was a spot of light which led me out of blackness. The blackness had engulfed the whole world, where I believed myself to be the only person alive.

Now the words on the screen
seemed to have been
edited and were describing a new state of being, where I was no longer frightened.

The rubber bands which had been tying my brain together seemed to have snapped. I must have gone to sleep then.

Another night, some time later, I found myself inside some kind of
being, where I heard a very quiet voice gradually becoming louder. Slowly it
became loud enough for me to recognise words
and to hear
someone talking to me. I appeared to be
inside a bubble, which was floating
gently about, but which seemed
strong enough to hold me safely.
The experience was more
tangible than a dream,
because I was sure I was awake.
I found myself downstairs, curled up on
the sofa, with a cup of tea
and listening to some soothing music.
I felt as though I had been turned inside out.

My Bundled Alphabet in 2003

I awoke in front of a mass of bundled letters from the alphabet.

    Carefully, by reading through, line by line, they formed a word which told me not to forget and in times of stress always to ask for help, instead of trying to cope by myself. The word, "REMEMBER", will always remain in my brain.

    The following night I awoke in a state of panic. I relived experiences from my past, which I am convinced I have stored somewhere in my brain, because they are too strong to die.

    They were devastating. I was forced to confront each one again. I was allowed no rest until I provided some kind of answer for each one.

abcdefghijklmnopqrstuvwxyz

defghijklmnopq**R**stuvwxyzabc

stuvwxyzabcd**E**fghijklmnopqr

xyzabcdefghijkl**M**nopqrstuvw

qrstuvwxyzabcd**E**fghijklmnop

vwxyzabcdefghijkl**M**nopqrstu

nopqrstuvwxyza**B**cdefghijklm

stuvwxyzabcd**E**fghijklmnopqrs

defghijklmnopq**R**stuvwxyzabc

abcdefghijklmnopqrstuvwxyz

Reality or Fantasy? in 2003

I forgot to take my pills last night and thought at first that must have been the reason for feeling so bad yesterday. But of course that didn't make sense because I'd forgotten them after the bad day, not before it. I had spent the whole day curled up on my sofa, with no energy to fulfil any appointments in my diary, even though some of them had been ones I'd been looking forward to.

This morning I was very surprised to wake up because I had been convinced I had died last night. I must have woken up in the middle of the night inside this strange state of fantasy. I made the decision that I must not strain myself because I was scared of tearing my muscles into shreds. But I was still emphatic about finding enough strength to go round the house to make sure everything was in the right place. Nothing I wanted to hide must be left in sight and nothing must be hidden that I was anxious to be found.

The whole time I was worrying about my cat being lonely without me, but reassured myself that my neighbours would look after her. Everything seemed to fit together as in a jig-saw puzzle. I tried to believe that I would be able to drift into a grave of mud. I focused on Ken's face smiling at me and trying to believe that he was watching me patiently, waiting for me to join him, wherever he was.

I didn't bother to get dressed because there seemed to be no reason. But at the same time another part of me was reminding me to be presentable for the visitor I was expecting. That gave me a shred of purpose. I was relieved to remember that I was expecting someone from the church to come round soon. I was very pleased to believe that he must be able to cope with my death and would find God somewhere to look after me when I disappeared from the world. He would help me believe there was some presence outside of myself.

I knew that I had been in this state before, but even so I was unable to reassure myself that I must have survived last time. If I had not, how could I be able to find myself still thinking? But nothing could be logical.

I was able to wonder how I could remember scraps from my past with no memory to do the work. I felt as though I was living in some place where everything had been turned inside out. The telephone rang and I started speaking to someone I had not had any contact with for a very long time. But I still remembered who he was and was able to make conversation with a blank person. Then I must have been able to go to sleep, because I found myself waking up. I forced myself to get up when I heard a sound downstairs It reminded me of the sound of the letterbox opening and I was relieved to realise that I must be in some contact with a reality that I recognised. The card that had fallen on the floor was from someone I had lost contact with, who explained to me that her father had died. I was reassured by this mention of death, so that I could make something regular with my terror of the unknown. The holes in my presence seemed to be filling up with faint memories.

While I was curled on the sofa, I saw an ambulance park itself outside my window, but nobody came out of it. I believed it had been sent to wait for the moment I would die. I was reassured that I would not be left to rot where nobody would notice I had died. But those moments of waiting would not stop and I was in a place of silence. Time seemed to progress forever and boredom seemed to enfold me.

Then I found myself able to glimpse something. I thought of the collection of memories I was putting together and I had to make sure that I had left my work in a place, obvious to be found by whoever would take over my task.

Now I start to write these words you are reading at this very moment. There is so much to express that I find it impossible to decide what is most important to record and what I can trust to find it's own way of remaining in the present. I feel like a bowl of gravel being tipped into dust. Some falls into the rubbish bin and some is left to rot on a path. Do I really want to remember my past, where I might meet some being whom I would really be better without.

I am scared of the present being so much better than the past, even when I still have to live alone, with these glimpses of trauma. I desperately need to be shaken out of this state, where I am disappearing into a fog, which may be covering nothing at all.

Remembering in 2003

I wake up in a mist of smiling faces. I realise they know me because of their expressions. Some of them may be friends from my past and some of them may be people I have loved very strongly. A few of them drive past, looking through their windows and waving.

I have not seen them for a very long time. I recognise some faces and even remember some names. The background of this vision has started very dark, then light slowly blends and grows gracefully into rich gold. The vision does not disappear, but gradually fades. I can wake up the next morning, get dressed, eat my breakfast, cry emotionally and carry on with my day.

Sometimes I feel very sad that I may never see past friends, but sometimes I feel enriched by the belief that there must be space in my heart for new friendship.

I need faith to remember that this vision has been here before. So I am glad to have recorded it on paper that is tangible and not merely to have let it fade away, lost in my memory, which is damaged.

SUPPORTING GILL
Val (2003)

Gill is an amazingly strong lady and it is easy to forget
how hard she works to maintain her independence and
to progress. I still have to remind myself that her
memory is really gone, even though it appears to be
improving. This is only due to her natural character and
her ability to find ways around her difficulties.

Gill has low days, when more help would be
beneficial, but the truth is that Gill does not remember.
So, unless it was instant and able to happen repeatedly,
it would be of no use. If someone or something is not
continuous or consistent in Gill's life it will simply
disappear.

Sympathy is no use to Gill, but understanding and
appreciation are beneficial.

FRIENDSHIP WITH GILL
Rosie (2003)

When I first met Gill I was working as an arts
Development officer for 'Artability South East'. I was
involved in running an arts project that offered private
tuition at home for disabled people. The project ended
with an arts exhibition in Brighton, which included Gill's
work.

   Gill wanted to keep contact and told me she wanted to
write about her experiences of Epilepsy, to help others
understand more about it. I agreed that I would have a
look at her work and see if I could help. She arrived at
our appointment with a bundle of papers, poems,
drawings and diaries, as well as a map to show her how to
get home again, even though she lived just five
minutes' walk from the office. She explained that she had
a damaged memory and that she would need to
photograph me in order to retain a link for our next
meeting. We also decided that I should take notes about
our conversation for her. We agreed that I would type her
handwritten manuscripts for her on the office computer.
She was unable to help because of the flickering of the
light on the screen. She kept coming to see me once a
week and we got on well, making sure that everything
was recorded, so that we didn't have to waste time going
over old ground. But she would still not recognise me
when she arrived. I dealt with this by stating who I was
and recapping on our last meeting in a very matter-of-
fact way.

   When Artability closed down in the Autumn, I had to
cancel our meeting by phoning her. She didn't have a
clue who I was, but when I explained about the work
we'd been doing, she apologised and invited me round for
a cup of tea. It was a very difficult experience for me to
arrive at her door as a complete stranger even then. We
realised later that she had not expected me to arrive early,
so she had not had a chance to look at my photograph
before I arrived.

As our weekly meetings progressed, we spent time together becoming friends, but she still relied on prompts to remember anything about the previous times.

When her work about her Epilepsy finished we wanted to remain friends, rather than me seeing her as just a past project.

We are good friends now and we have shared good times and bad, developing a way of being together in the NOW. We find we get excited about the same things, talk about life and gossip endlessly.

I have found her to be a friend who is caring, thoughtful, honest, fun to be with and intriguing to spend time with.

I know that things such as her taste, ideas, talent, intellect and common sense are consistent and she often returns to ideas we have shared as if they are brand new. I find this an affirmation of those ideas being a great deal to her and that she needs to keep exploring them.

I have helped her understand her computer and digital camera when frustration overwhelms her. This is often over the phone because she needs to follow up ideas quickly, before they fade and disappear.

She has helped me through difficult times by listening to me prattle on, providing me with tea and cakes and common sense.

A LOCAL VIEW OF GILLIAN
Mark (2003)

Ken introduced me to his friend Gillian several times. It was explained to me that Gillian, who was new to our village, had had a severe illness, which had left her with epilepsy and no memory whatsoever of her life prior to the illness. It concerned me that she had been thus afflicted, but having been apprised of the situation, it did not worry me at all that she often greeted me with "Do I know you? You'll have to tell me your name." It worried me more that she often lost herself, although, knowing the folk of Rusthall, I think most would have willingly pointed her in the right direction, even if they'd not done so before. Perhaps, if her condition had not been explained, some people may have thought it a bit odd to be asked the way to local places on more than one occasion. Those of us who knew Gill just accepted that was the way things were. Certainly I heard no one at all who considered it an affront not to be recognised. Nor have I ever heard anyone speak a bad word of Gillian, but rather the reverse.

It's been good to know that Gillian's medication has been so successful in reducing her epileptic seizures to a minimum. It's good also to be recognised now, although I realise that if we didn't meet for many weeks she may not recognise me next time. I would, however, recognise her, so it's no problem for me, although frustrating for her.

She and her friend Ken were, using modern parlance, "an item", which makes them sound something of an inventory! Those of us who'd known Ken for a long time were pleased that, after some years of widowhood, he found Gillian, who brought happiness in his final years. But this was clearly no one-sided dependent relationship. They were supportive of each other and we were pleased that these two very agreeable people had become close friends, to their mutual benefit.

There was a knock at my door about two years ago. It was our assistant curate. She was clearly upset and told me that Ken had died that morning. Apparently Gillian had found him. She urged me to call on Gillian sometime soon. I didn't do so immediately. It was, I felt, important not to go barging into her private grief, but left a note saying that I was thinking of her.

Gillian was, I am sure, grateful for the support she received from friends and neighbours, many of whom were associated with the church to which Ken had introduced her, but she soon began to allay our fears. We had underestimated this slender young woman, who seemed rather vulnerable . Not only did she cope, she coped very well.

We began to get to know her as herself, not just as Ken's friend. Here was a highly intelligent and talented person who was also very kind and possessed a great sense of humour. I fear that we had been so concerned to always take her seriously that we missed the twinkle in her eye. She is certainly very straightforward and doesn't hesitate to speak her mind, when the rest of us are too concerned about people's reactions to have her courage.

I think we are now able (to misquote Karl Barth's words about Mozart) to recognise Gillian's disability and affirm her ability, of which she has a great share. Probably she is doing the same herself, at least it looks that way. Gillian is positive. One of her positive things to record, is in writing about and photographing memories of her past. Having accepted the loss from her brain memory, she is now keeping a 'hard copy'.

Yes, we do worry about her at times. Some of us were rather concerned when she expressed a desire to get a bicycle, but she bought herself a memorable white one and a shed in which to house it. In no time at all Gillian was pedalling into Tonbridge Wells for her shopping, and to attend her Yoga classes, instead of relying on the local bus services. Now these of us with bicycles find ourselves accompanying her for rides into the countryside and are grateful to be given an excuse to leave mundane tasks in order to enjoy some fresh air, exercise, lovely views and good company.

From the physical to the spiritual, since Ken's death, Gillian has continued with her attendance at the local church's family service and become a very valued member of the congregation. She took the step of being baptised and later confirmed into the Church of England, the culmination of a process which had began with Ken's encouragement.

Gillian's illness can be regarded as a tragedy for her, her family and old friends. While fully acknowledging that, one can see it has had positive results too. Perhaps she and Ken would not have met, perhaps she would not have become a Christian, or moved to Rusthall. That would have left many of us all the poorer.

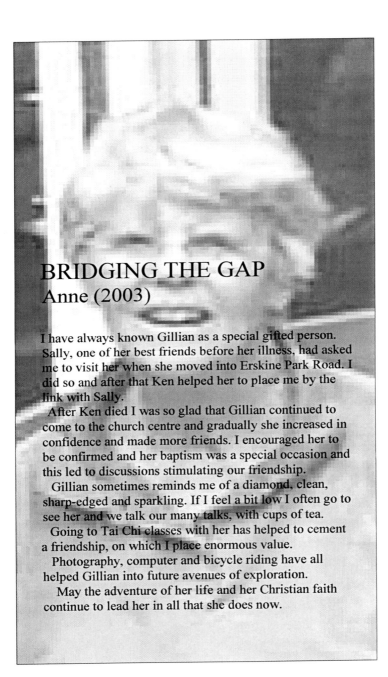

BRIDGING THE GAP
Anne (2003)

I have always known Gillian as a special gifted person. Sally, one of her best friends before her illness, had asked me to visit her when she moved into Erskine Park Road. I did so and after that Ken helped her to place me by the link with Sally.

After Ken died I was so glad that Gillian continued to come to the church centre and gradually she increased in confidence and made more friends. I encouraged her to be confirmed and her baptism was a special occasion and this led to discussions stimulating our friendship.

Gillian sometimes reminds me of a diamond, clean, sharp-edged and sparkling. If I feel a bit low I often go to see her and we talk our many talks, with cups of tea.

Going to Tai Chi classes with her has helped to cement a friendship, on which I place enormous value.

Photography, computer and bicycle riding have all helped Gillian into future avenues of exploration.

May the adventure of her life and her Christian faith continue to lead her in all that she does now.

WORKING WITH GILL
Pam (2003)

The first thing I noticed about Gill was her enthusiasm and her intense desire to learn. Gill came to COMPAID Trust after having been extremely ill and as a consequence suffered from extreme memory loss, as well as epilepsy. COMPAID Trust is a registered charity with a day to underestimate the extent of her difficulties and I certainly fell into the trap of assuming that it would be easy to teach her. However, it soon became apparent that Gill needed a variety of different strategies in order to learn.

At first it was an intense learning curve for both of us. For me it was because I found it almost impossible to visualise that I would have to teach her functions of the computer, then realise that within minutes, instructions would have completely slipped from her mind.

Gill is a delightful lady with a very strong will and at first she was determined to try to use her memory without any notes. This, as you can imagine, led to some heated discussions!

Over a period of time, Gill and I worked together successfully on a variety of projects. Gill is a very artistic lady. At COMPAID Trust she has created posters, photo montages and over a period of time, has learned PC skills which have helped her produce projects like this one. At last, she has accepted the need for strategies and supplements to assist her memory. For example, she has learned to use a laptop computer with a digital camera to assist her memory.

I really enjoy the challenge of working with Gill and through her I have learned more patience and new ways to teach!

AN INSPIRING PERSON
Rob (2004)

I knew Gill from church and was aware that she had
Epilepsy and memory difficulties. We often said hello
at church but never normally said more than a few
words.

One Sunday we got talking and Gillian gave me a
booklet that she had produced, "Now Then Epilepsy".
It gave me a glimpse of Gillian's struggle to lead a
normal life, and I was inspired.

Two years later I asked her if I could use her booklet
as the focus of my talk at Family Service. She said yes,
that she wanted people to be aware and understand
epilepsy, that's why she produced the booklet and
could she help.

I was pleased she was OK with it. I was even more
pleased when she offered to help, after all Gillian was
the expert on epilepsy, she had lived with it for
twenty- one years.

I suggested we got together a couple of times to
make sure I knew what I was talking about. That
turned into ten or twelve meetings lasting two, sometimes three hours. I guess that was when we became
friends.

For the talk, Gillian spent hours putting together her
thoughts, pictures and poems and extracts from her
diaries.

She wanted to stand up and say the last part of the
talk, but felt she would be too nervous and unable to.
She did though.

MY SISTER
Patricia (2004)

Reading Gill's book as her sister, who has lived through the long period of her illness and recovery, I recognise the truth of the narrative in terms of the flow of her experience. Yet there is something missing. What?

I would say that what 'recovery' has meant, looking at Gill's life from the outside over more than twenty years since the Encephilitis virus struck, is the return of continuity, the kind of background rhythm of living, working and relating that the rest of us take for granted.

Gill's story misses out the periods when her fits so incapacitated her that normal life and experience were suspended for a while. She really needed a lot of support. She would 'recover' each time, but she could not progress. Because these periods were like patches of dark between the windows of her intelligent consciousness, she has joined the windows together to make a smooth journey out of what, from my perspective, was a roller-coaster ride. Each time she built up some continuity, it was destroyed again by a bad cluster of fits.

Since finding, during the last eight years, a drug that at last has stopped these terrible times, she has managed to create what we all need – a real community of friends, the ability to sustain and achieve activities she wants, a pattern of life in which she recognises herself and is recognised by others in a consistent way. Despite fits continuing and the past always fading of memories not regularly renewed, she has gained once more a real identity after a long struggle.

•

Even Now in 2004

Losing my bicycle

I lost my bicycle last week, even though I had left it in what I'm
sure was the usual place, where I'm confident it is always safe.
When I returned for it, along familiar roads, it had disappeared,
even though I had locked it up carefully. After some fruitless
searches around this place and a visit to the police station to
register it's disappearance, I went back home on the bus, feeling
tired and depressed.

I found it the following day, by carefully retracing my
route - the direction into town, not back home. It was standing
where I expected, looking lonely, as though I had abandoned it. I
realised that yesterday I had not been concentrating enough to
cycle in the right direction. All the buildings on busy roads look
the same to me, especially if I don't bother to register signposts.

In everything I do, I must be very careful to store details,
which allow me to have confidence in where I am or what I am
doing. Getting lost can happen to us all, but I am always
confronted by that state, however many times I experience the
simplest of journeys.

Losing Friends

People I meet sometimes want to find out more about my
damaged memory because the condition is new to them. At first
they often dismiss it with a laugh as something we all have to experience as we get older. But my memory is much weaker and
parts of it are already dead. If anyone wants to make friends with
me they must not be daunted by the hard work it appears to need.

I often forget friends' faces completely and usually their
names. I often forget conversations and events we shared last
time we met, however recent they are and however good or
important they may have been. This can cause irritation,
misunderstanding and hurt. People may feel that I am asking too
much from them, or that I am rubbing them out of my life with
no acknowledgement or respect for what they may have already
offered.

It is very difficult to find a pace that is comfortable for us both.
I need faith in friendship. I do not know strong roots for it to
grow from, but friendship with me can still bloom and blossom.
It just needs to be watered regularly.

RELAX!

Lie down flat upon the floor
with no one else here anymore.
This feels so good and so it should
when bad times have been here today.
Think of yourself, both mind and body;
believe you really are somebody;
one who matters, one who shatters,
where peace can really let you pray.
Think of your toes, think of your ankles,
think of your knees, think of your thighs,
think of your back, think of your chest,
think of your arms, your wrists, your fingers
think of your nose, your eyes and brain
and anything else that causes stress.
Find peace!
Be happy to live in the present!
(GS 2004)

A SIMPLE CHRONOLOGY by my sister

1954 Gill was born.

1972 Gill studied a foundation course in art.

1973 Gill went to Bristol Polytechnic to study graphic design.

1976 Gill went to the Royal College of Art in London to study Graphic Design of information.

1978 Gill set up a graphic design partnership called 'Information Design Workshop' in Docklands, in the outskirts of London.

1982 After Encephalitis struck her, Gill struggled to lead a relatively independent life back in her own house.

1990 Gill moved in briefly with me and my husband.

1991 Gill experienced some traumatic relationships which nearly led her to having breakdowns.

1995 Social Services helped to find a Housing Association house for her in Rusthall and introduced her to a number of new activities.

1996 Gill started taking a more effective drug treatment. She also met Ken Smith, who became a close friend and introduced her to more friends and to the local church.

2000 Gill started doing more inspiring design work at COMPAID, becoming involved in learning to combine the computer with her graphic skills.

2003 Gill was baptised and confirmed by Canon Bob Whyte at St.Paul's Church, Rusthall.

2004 Gill discovered she could still ride a bicycle.